D1406057

Mothers and Daughters

for Melanie —

best wishes,

Liza

June 1993

Mothers and Daughters

Edited by Liza Donnelly

Ballantine Books • New York

Sale of this book without a front cover may be unauthorized. If this book is coverless, it may have been reported to the publisher as "unsold or destroyed" and neither the author nor the publisher may have received payment for it.

Introduction and compilation
Copyright © 1993 by Liza Donnelly

Copyright to individual cartoons is retained by the artist or as otherwise noted.

All rights reserved under International and Pan-American Copyright Conventions. Published in the United States by Ballantine Books, a division of Random House, Inc., New York, and simultaneously in Canada by Random House of Canada Limited, Toronto.

Library of Congress Catalog Card Number: 92-93453

ISBN: 0-345-38361-3

Cover illustration by Liza Donnelly

Manufactured in the United States of America
First Edition: May 1993
10 9 8 7 6 5 4 3 2

INTRODUCTION

There is something about mothers and daughters. Everyone knows a pair. Either they *are* one—a mother of a daughter or a daughter of a mother—or they are married to a pair; are brother to a pair; or are simply friends of a pair.

This relationship is often a love-hate thing, a hate-hate thing, or even a love-love thing. It can be a humorous thing. At least that's how the cartoonists in this anthology feel. In these drawings, one glimpses the inside of this unique relationship between two women, one a daughter and one a mother. All the contributors herein are either one or the other—or both!

For the last three and a half years, I have spent most of my time trying to understand my two young daughters, and trying to understand how to be a mother. I thought about my own mother, my stepmother, my stepmother's daughters, my sister's daughter, my husband's mother, my friends' mothers, and my friends' daughters . . . and all this reflection led to the birth of the book you now hold.

It has been enjoyable compiling *Mothers and Daughters,* and I thank all the contributors for their enthusiasm and ideas. I'd also like to thank their mothers, their daughters, their stepmothers, their sisters' daughters, their husbands' mothers, their lovers' mothers, their daughters' sisters, and their mothers' mothers . . .

— Liza Donnelly

P.S.   And of course I would like to thank my daughters, my mother, my editor, and my husband.

Mothers and Daughters

Sherrie Shepherd

Teresa McCracken

"*I'm conversing for two.*"

Victoria Roberts

"I should warn you now, we Wagner women
have always had pear-shaped bodies."

Donna Barstow

Anne Gibbons

Gail Machlis

WHERE I'M COMING FROM

BY BARBARA BRANDON

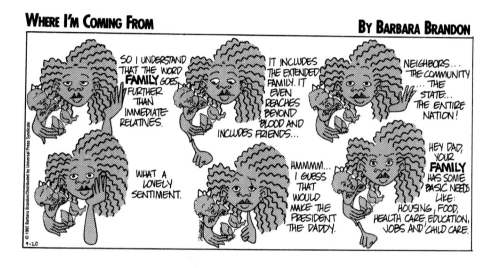

SO I UNDERSTAND THAT THE WORD **FAMILY** GOES FURTHER THAN IMMEDIATE RELATIVES.

IT INCLUDES THE EXTENDED FAMILY. IT EVEN REACHES BEYOND BLOOD AND INCLUDES FRIENDS...

NEIGHBORS... THE COMMUNITY ... THE STATE... THE ENTIRE NATION!

WHAT A LOVELY SENTIMENT.

HMMMM... I GUESS THAT WOULD MAKE THE PRESIDENT THE DADDY.

HEY DAD, YOUR **FAMILY** HAS SOME BASIC NEEDS LIKE: HOUSING, FOOD, HEALTH CARE, EDUCATION, JOBS AND CHILD CARE.

© 1992 Barbara Brandon/Distributed by Universal Press Syndicate

9-20

Where I'm Coming From Copyright 1992 Barbara Brandon.
Dist. by Universal Press Syndicate.
Reprinted with permission. All rights reserved

"...and you mocked me
when I played Bartók to her in the womb."

Gail Machlis

Liza Donnelly

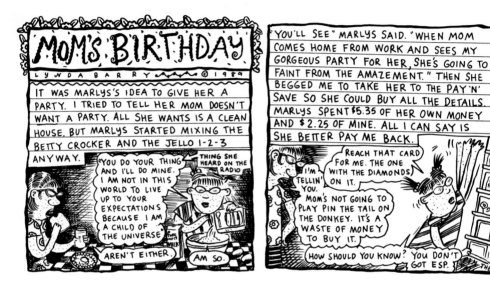

MOM'S BIRTHDAY

LYNDA BARRY © 1989

IT WAS MARLYS'S IDEA TO GIVE HER A PARTY. I TRIED TO TELL HER MOM DOESN'T WANT A PARTY. ALL SHE WANTS IS A CLEAN HOUSE. BUT MARLYS STARTED MIXING THE BETTY CROCKER AND THE JELLO 1-2-3 ANYWAY.

"YOU DO YOUR THING AND I'LL DO MINE. I AM NOT IN THIS WORLD TO LIVE UP TO YOUR EXPECTATIONS BECAUSE I AM A CHILD OF THE UNIVERSE"

THING SHE HEARD ON THE RADIO

AREN'T EITHER.

AM SO.

"YOU'LL SEE" MARLYS SAID. "WHEN MOM COMES HOME FROM WORK AND SEES MY GORGEOUS PARTY FOR HER, SHE'S GOING TO FAINT FROM THE AMAZEMENT." THEN SHE BEGGED ME TO TAKE HER TO THE PAY 'N' SAVE SO SHE COULD BUY ALL THE DETAILS. MARLYS SPENT $5.35 OF HER OWN MONEY AND $2.25 OF MINE. ALL I CAN SAY IS SHE BETTER PAY ME BACK.

REACH THAT CARD FOR ME. THE ONE WITH THE DIAMONDS ON IT.

I'M TELLIN' YOU.

MOM'S NOT GOING TO PLAY PIN THE TAIL ON THE DONKEY. IT'S A WASTE OF MONEY TO BUY IT.

HOW SHOULD YOU KNOW? YOU DON'T GOT E.S.P.

AT FIVE O'CLOCK, EVERYTHING WAS DONE. AND I HAVE TO ADMIT, IT LOOKED GOOD. I HAVE TO ADMIT EVEN I WAS EXCITED. THERE WAS 32 BALLOONS, GERMAN CHOCOLATE CAKE WITH CANDLES, ORANGE HI-C, THE JELLO DEALS, AND A SIGN: "HAPPY BIRTHDAY MOM" ON A LONG ROW OF PAPER TOWELS THAT LOOKED VERY ARTISTIC.

THERES HER CAR!!

NO, WAIT. FAKE-OUT.

HELP ME STICK THE REST OF THE PLASTIC SWORDS IN THE MARSH-MELLOWS.

AND I TURNED OUT TO BE WRONG. SHE DID WANT A PARTY. "YOU KIDS, YOU KIDS" SHE SAID WHEN SHE OPENED THE DOOR, AND SHE PICKED MARLYS UP AND STARTED TO CRY. THEN I STARTED TO CRY. THEN MARLYS STARTED TO CRY. AND I'LL ALWAYS REMEMBER THAT NIGHT AS A PERFECT NIGHT. A PERFECT NIGHT WHEN I SAW HER HAPPY.

AM I COLD OR HOT?

C'MON YOU GUYS. TELL ME.

First Printed by Harper Collins copyright Lynda Barry 1989.

Kathryn LeMieux

Nurit Karlin

Roz Chast

" We're very different."

Victoria Roberts

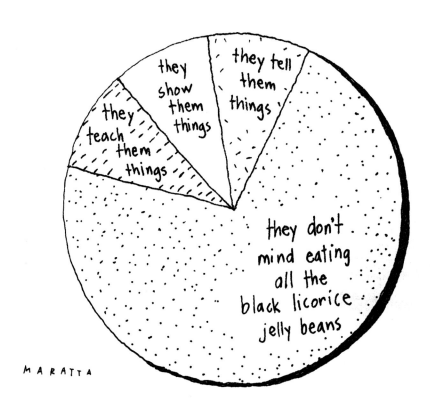

Why DAUGHTERS LOVE THEIR MOMMIES
a pie chart

they tell them things

they show them things

they teach them things

they don't mind eating all the black licorice jelly beans

MARATTA

Katie Maratta

The ultimate reply

Nurit Karlin

Corinne

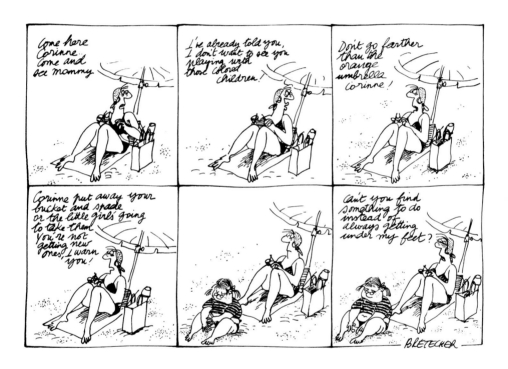

**Claire Bretecher, from _Frustration_, Methuen London.
Reprinted by permission of Methuen London.**

For Better or For Worse

By Lynn Johnston

For Better or for Worse 1984, 1985 & 1988 copyright Lynn Johnston Prod., Inc.
Reprinted with permission of Universal Press Syndicate. All rights reserved.

"*You mean she married the prince after only one date?*"

Martha Campell

Katie Maratta

Kathryn LeMieux

*"I don't need a bath today.
You can just vacuum me."*

Sandy Dean

Gail Machlis

Copyright © 1982, 1991 by Lynn Johnston Productions, Inc., and Lynn Johnston. Reprinted from *David, We're Pregnant!* with the permission of its publisher, Meadowbrook Press.

THE HAIRDRYER WARS

Ann McCarthy

*"And when I grow up, mom,
I want to be as beautiful as you."*

Huguette Martel

Woman, wife, mother, spin doctor

Katie Maratta

Debra Solomon

MOM-O-GRAMS

Drawing by R. Chast; © **1986 The New Yorker Magazine, Inc.**

Kathryn LeMieux

DONNELLY

*"This would be an opportune moment
to express yourself, dear."*

Liza Donnelly

U·G·L·I·F·U·L

BY LYNDA BARRY © 1989

THE FIRST THING ABOUT MY MOM IS THAT SHE WAS VERY BEAUTIFUL WHEN SHE WAS YOUNG. IN FACT, GORGEOUS. THE GORGEOUS TWIN OF AVA GARDNER, EVERYBODY SAID IT. MY MOM HAS TOLD US THIS 10,000 TIMES.

AND DID YOU KNOW I HAD WHAT THEY CONSIDERED PERFECT EYEBROWS?

WELL, IT'S ALL GONE TO HELL NOW. WASTED. SHOWS YOU WHAT HAVING KIDS CAN DO TO YOU.

SHE WAS SO BEAUTIFUL, FIVE GUYS ASKED HER TO MARRY THEM BEFORE SHE PICKED MY FATHER, THE WORST MISTAKE OF HER LIFE. I ALWAYS WONDER WHAT I COULD HAVE LOOKED LIKE INSTEAD, IF SHE HAD PICKED ONE OF THEM.

HERMAN KOSARSKI
LOOKED LIKE PERRY COMO

DAVID R. GAVLAK
NOW OWNS "GAVLAK SANITATION"

PETER FERRARA
BOY COULD HE DANCE.

WAYNE SHIPLEY
LOOKED LIKE "MAVERICK"

WILBERT BRUTOUT
NOW OWNS "BRUTOUT TEXACO"

WHEN I WAS LITTLE, I LOOKED JUST LIKE HER. WE HAD THOSE DRESSES THAT MATCH AND ACCORDING TO MY MOTHER, THE PEOPLE WHO SAW US SAID WE WERE WONDERFUL. THEN I HAD TO GET GLASSES WHICH MY MOTHER HATED BECAUSE IT SPOILED MY LOOKS. THIS WAS A LONG TIME AGO WHEN MY MOM'S EYES WERE PERFECT AND MY DAD WAS STILL WITH US.

MY BABY SISTER MARLYS WHO MY MOM SAYS WAS BORN WEARING GLASSES. AND ALSO "CHUBBY"

"YOU GOT YOUR FATHER'S LOOKS. THE BOTH OF YOU." SHE SAYS TO ME AND MY SISTER WHEN SHE GETS IN THAT ONE TALKING MOOD ABOUT HER MISTAKES IN LIFE. AND SHE TELLS ME I HAD BETTER GET BUSY WORKING ON MY CHARM. "WELL, BE GRATEFUL YOU DON'T HAVE A WEIGHT PROBLEM." SHE SAYS, THEN LOOKS STRAIGHT AT MY SISTER.

First Printed by Harper Collins copyright Lynda Barry 1989.

"Is that a 'don't bother me' no,
a 'maybe' no, or a 'no' no?"

Brenda Burbank

*"I bet if they'd called all the King's women
they could have put Humpty Dumpty together."*

Theresa McCracken

For Better or For Worse By Lynn Johnston

ELIZABETH, IF YOU WANT TO SEE YOUR HAIR IN PONYTAILS, YOU'LL HAVE TO SIT STILL!!

BUT... I DON'T WANT TO SEE MY HAIR IN PONY-TAILS.

YOU DO!

2-24

Lynn

For Better or for Worse 1984, 1985 & 1988 copyright Lynn Johnston Prod., Inc.
Reprinted with permission of Universal Press Syndicate. All rights reserved.

"Just remember, dear, being cute is half the battle."

M.K. Brown

"Mother, do you remember the first time <u>you</u> were stung by criticism?"

Liza Donnelly

Kathryn LeMieux

For Better or for Worse 1984, 1985 & 1988 copyright Lynn Johnston Prod., Inc.
Reprinted with permission of Universal Press Syndicate. All rights reserved.

DORIS K. ELSTON

BRAIN SURGEON·PROFESSIONAL
MODEL·ARTIST·LAWYER·
plus
MOTHER OF FOUR

Drawing by R. Chast; ©1987 The New Yorker Magazine, Inc.

Signe Wilkinson

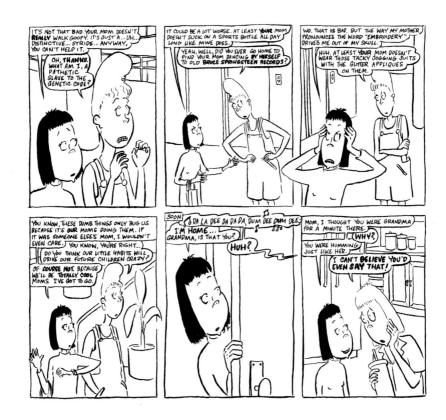

Mimi Pond

SYLVIA

by Nicole Hollander

MA, WHEN ARE YOU COMING OUT?

WHO'S THERE?

IT'S YOUR DAUGHTER, THE ONE WHO WOULD LIKE TO TAKE A SHOWER.

IF YOU'RE MY DAUGHTER, WHAT'S MY FAVORITE COLOR?

HOT PINK.

LUCKY GUESS. WHO'S MY FAVORITE MEMBER OF THE ROYAL FAMILY?

Nicole Hollander

*"I rebelled, too, Darla, back
when rebellion meant something."*

Liza Donnelly

Maxinel Comix © Marian Henley

I'm there if she needs me, but I try not to interfere.

I tell her everything, and she gives me really good advice.

NEXT ON OPRAH: Mothers and daughters who are actually speaking to each other

MARATTA

Katie Maratta

Our **Mothers** our **Selves**.
An insightful and thought-provoking look into female bonding.

Every woman is a miniature version of her mother.

As you get older and mature, you'll find this to be true.

Along lifes' twisted path, she will impart her sage wisdom, and you will heed her sound advice.

Soon you will start to behave in strange and mysterious ways, and think odd thoughts.

Your mother will always be on your mind, like a top 40 song played on the radio OVER and OVER and OVER again!

One day, when you have a girl of your own, you will appreciate and value all the knowledge your mother has taught you, and she'll be the wiser for it.

Stephanie Skalisky

Debra Solomon

EVE'S MOM

Drawing by R. Chast; ©1992 The New Yorker Magazine, Inc.

Trots and Bonnie

Shary Flenniken

Signe Wilkinson

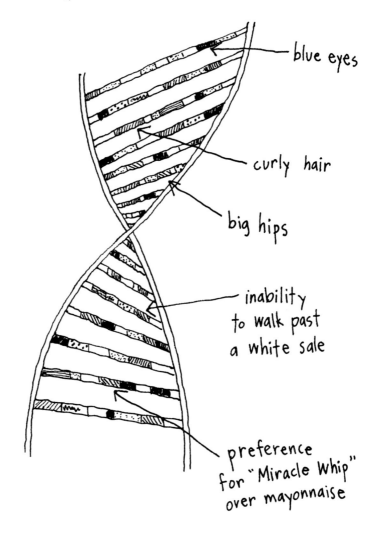

GENE MAP:
mother-to-daughter
inherited traits

blue eyes

curly hair

big hips

inability
to walk past
a white sale

preference
for "Miracle Whip"
over mayonnaise

MARATTA

Katie Maratta

SYLVIA

by Nicole Hollander

Hi, MOM. NO, MOM, WATCHING "MURPHY BROWN" HASN'T MADE ME WANT TO BE A SINGLE MOTHER OR A T.V. REPORTER OR AN ACTRESS.

© 1992 BY NICOLE HOLLANDER

IT DID MAKE ME ENVIOUS OF CANDICE BERGEN... HAVING A WOODEN DUMMY AS A BROTHER,

RATHER THAN THE ONE I HAVE... OF COURSE I'M KIDDING, MOM. I WORSHIP BILLY.

6-27
nicole Hollander

Nicole Hollander

ADVICE FOR THE **MODERN BRIDE:** PHOTO SESSION ETIQUETTE

1. Bride 2. Groom 3. Groom's daughter from first marriage 4. Bride's mother 5. Bride's mother's current lover 6. Bride's sperm donor father 7.&8. Sperm donor's parents who sued for visitation rights to bride 8. Bride's mother's lover at time of bride's birth 9. Bride's mother's lover at time of bride's birth 10. Groom's mother 11. Groom's mother's boyfriend 12. Groom's father 13. Groom's stepmother 14. Groom's father's third wife 15. Groom's grandfather 16. Groom's grandfather's lover 17. Groom's first wife

Signe Wilkinson

cathy®

by Cathy Guisewite

Cathy copyright 1988 Cathy Guisewite.
Reprinted with permission of Universal Press Syndicate.
All rights reserved.

THINGS YOUR MOTHER TOLD YOU
THAT WENT IN ONE EAR & STRAIGHT INTO YOUR SUBCONSCIOUS

Libby Reid

Which describes your relationship with your mother?

Moth
to
Flame

Moth
to
Other Moth

Moth
to
Wool Sweater

ZZZAP!

Moth
to
BUG ZAPPER

MARATTA

Katie Maratta

What did your mother think of your high school boyfriends?

After my first date, my mother told me she had three things to say about the guy I went out with...

He arrived late. He didn't wear a tie. And he walked on the INSIDE when we went down the block.

Needless to say, I went out with him for the next five years.

© Anne Gibbons

Anne Gibbons

Donna Barstow

Maxinel Comix © Marian Henley

Copyright Carol Tyler 1993.

Visit to mom.

Gail Machlis

cathy®

I'VE BEEN INVOLVED IN HUNDREDS OF EXCITING PROJECTS ALL YEAR.... AT MY MOTHER'S HOUSE, I SLUMP ON THE COUCH AND WATCH TV.

I'VE TRAVELED, READ, LEARNED, GROWN.... AT MOM'S HOUSE, I SLUMP ON THE COUCH AND WATCH TV.

I'VE ELEVATED MY PERSPECTIVE AND EXPANDED MY VISION IN A THOUSAND WAYS.... AT MOM'S HOUSE, I SLUMP ON THE COUCH AND WATCH TV.

I BROUGHT HOME A WHOLE NEW MENTAL WARDROBE, BUT ALL I EVER LET HER SEE IS MY MENTAL SWEATSUIT.

Cathy copyright 1988 Cathy Guisewite.
Reprinted with permission of Universal Press Syndicate.
All rights reserved.

"I love my mother, I love her not...."

Donna Barstow

Roz Chast

SYLVIA

by Nicole Hollander

Hi, Mom. Am I watching the reruns of that series on the Civil War? No, I didn't want to see it the first time, don't want to see it now.

2-4

Am I going to read the sequel to "Gone with the Wind"? Nope. I can tell you're disappointed. Is there something else I can do to make you happy?

© 1992 BY NICOLE HOLLANDER

Married? Sure, I'll do it this afternoon.

"By the way, how is your mom?"

Catherine Siracusa

"You said you wanted me
to marry someone like dad."

Sherrie Shepherd

Anne Gibbons

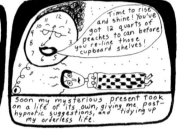

S. Skalisky

Stephanie Skalisky

Donna Barstow

Like Mutha, like dotter.

Heather McAdams

"But mama, a little balsamic vinegar and a few sundried tomatoes can only improve your recipe."

Catherine Siracusa

"My daughter and I often travel together.
I take her on guilt trips all the time."

Sherrie Shepherd

SYLVIA

by Nicole Hollander

When women with Figure Flaws Get their own Fairy Godmother.

Nicole Hollander 1-16

Stand up straight, honey... what can I do for you?

A woman can have her nose or her breasts surgically altered, but if you're cursed with small shoulders, there's no hope.

SHAZAM!

Are you happy?

Now my head looks small.

©1992 By Nicole Hollander

Nicole Hollander

cathy®

by Cathy Guisewite

Panel 1:
WHY HAVEN'T YOU ASKED ABOUT IRVING, MOM?

I THOUGHT I WASN'T SUPPOSED TO ASK ABOUT IRVING ANYMORE.

Panel 2:
NO. YOU WEREN'T SUPPOSED TO ASK ABOUT IRVING WHEN I WAS SEEING MITCH...YOU'RE NOT SUPPOSED TO ASK ABOUT MITCH ANYMORE...AND YOU'RE NEVER SUPPOSED TO ASK ABOUT ANYONE I'VE MENTIONED LESS THAN THREE TIMES OR MORE THAN SIX WEEKS AGO...

Panel 3:
...BUT NOW I WANT YOU TO ASK ABOUT IRVING! I'VE BEEN HOPING YOU'D ASK!!

Panel 4:
EVERY TIME I THINK I'M GETTING A GRIP ON THE JOB, SHE REVISES THE TRAINING MANUAL.

Cathy copyright 1988 Cathy Guisewite.
Reprinted with permission of Universal Press Syndicate.
All rights reserved.

*"Just a brief reminder, mother: both times
I married, I married a Larry. This is the second Larry."*

Liza Donnelly

SYLVIA

*"I'm sorry, sir, but there's nothing much
I can do about it. It's a mother-daughter thing."*

Donna Barstow

"Here's one your mother would
certainly disapprove of."

Liza Donnelly

A MOTHER'S STRUGGLE

Claire Bretecher, from *Frustration*, Methuen London.
Reprinted by permission of Methuen London.

Maxinel Comix © **Marian Henley**

Jennifer Berman

Heredity

Nurit Karlin

SYLVIA ON SUNDAY

by Nicole Hollander

Nicole Hollander

*"Mother still loves it
when people think we're sisters."*

Sherrie Shepherd

For Better or for Worse 1984, 1985 & 1988 copyright Lynn Johnston Prod., Inc.
Reprinted with permission of Universal Press Syndicate. All rights reserved.